NOW YOU CAN READ...
DAVID and GOLIATH

STORY RETOLD BY ELAINE IFE

ILLUSTRATED BY ERIC ROWE

THOMAS NELSON PUBLISHERS · NASHVILLE · CAMDEN · NEW YORK

Copyright © 1982 by Brimax Rights, Inc.

David was a shepherd boy. He looked
after his father's sheep. He had to
see that no one came to steal the
sheep. If a wild animal came close,
he had to chase it away. David had
seven brothers. He was the youngest
in the family.

One day, as he was
tending the sheep in
the field, he saw
someone coming. He
jumped up and ran
to meet him. It
was one of his
father's servants.

The servant said, "Leave the sheep, David. Come back to your father's house. Someone wants to see you. I will look after the sheep while you are gone."

David ran quickly to the house.

His face was red as he ran inside.

His father was standing next to
another man, and said to David,
"This man is called Samuel. He
wants to meet you. He has a
special job for you to do."

Samuel knew that when David grew up, he would be the king of the country. He was still a boy, but God had told Samuel that David was His choice for the next king. Samuel put oil on David's head to show he was God's choice.

Samuel talked to David and then he went away.

At that time, the king of the country was a man called Saul. He was not a very good king. Sometimes he felt unhappy and would not speak to anyone. "Perhaps if someone played some cheerful music for King Saul, it would make him feel happy," said one of the servants.

David could play lovely music on the harp. He was asked to go to the palace and play for King Saul. He played some happy music and sang songs and soon the King was more cheerful.

"I want you to stay here at the palace," said King Saul. "Send a message to your father to tell him where you are."

David liked being at the palace. He talked to the King about his home and the lambs in the fields. Soon after David had gone to the palace, war broke out. King Saul had to get his army ready.

Three of David's brothers were in the army, so he had to go back to his father.

One day, David took some new bread to his brothers. He liked to go and see the soldiers.

David was talking to
his brothers when
a great shout was
heard. A huge man,
a giant, was walk-
ing towards
them.

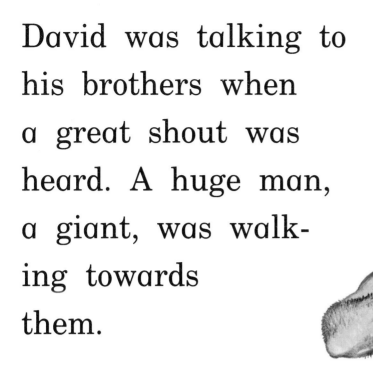

"Who will fight
with me?" he roared.
"If he wins, then
you have won this
battle, but if I
win, then you will
all be in our
power."

"Who is going to fight him?" asked
David.

"No one dares to fight Goliath,"
said one of the soldiers. "No one
could stand up to a man like that."
David knew at once what he should
do. He went to King Saul.

"I will fight Goliath," he said.
"You!" cried King Saul. "You are only a youth. Goliath is a real fighter. You cannot fight him."
"I may be small," said David, "but with God's help I have killed bears and lions when they came to steal my father's sheep. Please, let me try."

King Saul took off the suit of
armour which he was wearing and put
it on David. It was much too big.
He tripped over it.

"I cannot wear this," said David.
"It is too heavy and too big.
Please take it off." The armour
was taken off and David felt much
better.

He took his sling
and went to a
little stream
nearby. He chose
five smooth stones
and put them in
a bag. Then he
walked towards the
giant.

Goliath could not believe his eyes. A little boy was coming to fight him! He put down his great head and charged. David took one of the stones out of his bag and put it in his sling.

He spun the sling around his head, faster and faster and let it go.

The stone flew through the air and hit Goliath right in the middle of his forehead. He crashed to the ground like a fallen tree.

David ran up to him and took the sword from Goliath's side. With one blow, he cut off Goliath's head. All the soldiers cheered and shouted. The enemy turned and ran away.

King Saul spoke to David. "You shall stay with us now. You will not return to your father's house. My son, Jonathan, will be a good friend to you."

Jonathan was very kind to David and they became like brothers.

All these appear in the pages of
the story. Can you find them?

David

sheep

King Saul

Samuel